THE KOOL-AID DISPENSER

By the same author:

Fiction

Glissando: A Melodrama (2010)
The Obituary Collector (2025)

Poetry

To Thalia (2004)
On Reflection (2005)
Watermark (2006)
Open Water (Audio CD) (2007)
Phantom Limb (2010)
Concrete Tuesday (2011)
Anatomy of Voice (2016)
Numb & Number (2019)
Selected Poems (2021)
Numb & Number (Audio CD) (2021)
Mishearing (2023)
Anatomy of Voice (Audio CD) (2024)

Non-fiction

Grotesque Anatomies: Menippean Satire since the Renaissance (2014)

Edited

Contemporary Australian Poetry
(ed. With M. Langford, J. Beveridge & J. Johnson) (2015)
Feeding the Ghost 1 (ed. With A. Kissane & C. Rickett) (2018)

THE KOOL-AID DISPENSER

DAVID MUSGRAVE

RECENT
WORK
PRESS
2015-2025
10 YEARS OF POETRY

The Kool-Aid Dispenser
Recent Work Press
Canberra, Australia

Copyright © David Musgrave, 2025

ISBN: 9781763670150 (paperback)

 A catalogue record for this book is available from the National Library of Australia

All rights reserved. This book is copyright. Except for private study, research, criticism or reviews as permitted under the Copyright Act, no part of this book may be reproduced, stored in a retrieval system, or transmitted in any form by any means without prior written permission. Enquiries should be addressed to the publisher.

Cover design: Recent Work Press
Set by Recent Work Press

This book was written on the unceded lands of the Pambalong clan of the Awabakal nation.

recentworkpress.com
10 YEARS OF POETRY

MD JL

给京禧

Contents

THE KOOL-AID

Letter to a Dead Parent	5
Western Elegies: Three Ways Home	7
In Memory of Ross Hannaford	11
Ando at the Sando	13
The Poet's Wake	14
Halfway Things	16

DIAL 0, OK?

Parthenope	21
The Excursion	22
Dynamics of Reason	24
Monotudes	25
Constant Trembling	26
Shy Architecture	27

KOOL-AID DISPENSERS

The Dawson Twins	31
Achtung Baby	32
I Make Northrop Frye Laugh, 1986	33
Ode to the Manifest Image	34
The Earth	37
The Answer	38
The History of Violence	45

KOELS TO NEWCASTLE

Five Puddles	49
Milk Teeth	50
Walking with my young son I remember I am only a year shy of the age my father was when he had his fatal stroke	51
苏轼《洗儿诗》Su Shi 'Washing my Son'	53
Arborealism	54
Kooragang Dawdn	55
Warabrook Wetlands	56
Food Poisoning, Red Rooster, Waratah	58
Three pigeons	59
Koels to Newcastle	60
Jingxitude	61
How I love thunderstorms:	62

—Whose was it?
His who is gone.
—Who shall have it?
He who will come.
—What was the month?
The sixth from the first.
—What shall we give for it?
All that is ours.
—Why should we give it?
For the sake of the trust.

Arthur Conan Doyle, 'The Adventure of the Musgrave Ritual'

Thomas: Who shall have it?
Tempter: He who will come.
Thomas: What shall be the month?
Tempter: The last from the first.
Thomas: What shall we give for it?
Tempter: Pretence of priestly power.
Thomas: Why should we give it?
Tempter: For the power and the glory.

T.S. Eliot, *Murder in the Cathedral*

THE KOOL-AID

Letter to a Dead Parent

Whenever I look at your grandson,
I see dad's face, but you're the one
or several parts of one, who animates his rage
and cheek, just as how the other day
at two-and-a-quarter, he put a soccer ball
into a bucket and called it 'ice cream', licking it.
It's as if you're still alive, but blind to survival,
counting 'one, two, five, eighteen, twenty four'
with the precision of a train timetable
opened at random. How you would have loved
to see him, even in your last unravelling,
the way he pushes away my hand
if I try to turn the page too soon, or how
he will stare blankly ahead, ignoring anything
I say before slyly looking sideways at me,
then laughing. It's hard to believe
that part of me could go on being, let alone
this tenacious chain that links to you, here,
where a breeze bends the corridor
around its cold and touches your hair.
A lot has happened since you've gone:
this pandemic; it's strange how there
are no individuals, just a society where
you can hide but can't run.
Your grandson brings me a horse's head
in the palm of his hand, separated from its body
by an accident, and overcome by penitence,
says 'sorry daddy' over and over, lying face down
on the ground. I didn't teach him this,

so where did he learn it? I'm sorry that you never got to see
his frown, breathing over a shark or Boss Choongus
in the Big House at the end of the road.
But when he points at agave plants
along the side path, tells me 'dinosaur',
I think of dying, of sores,
am reminded of old saws
and older truths, the hardening of bone
or its mirror, sagging skin, a voice that's broken
into words, or words flowering into the wave
of his hand, 'goodbye outside, goodbye diningsaur'.

Western Elegies: Three Ways Home

1. The Fitzroy River

In the wet this river lashes out
across the plain, a standing wave of water
out to sea. Days darken in mudsquall
boiling around taproot lightning. Levees

churn apart, the river slaps them together
again and everything sinks into clay.
All that is born returns to country,
baby freshwater crocs, gunmetal-grey,

vast shoals of cloud swimming up from the Pilbara,
and you. The cherubin left here years ago,
you said, and now less fish, but a pain in your side
that nothing could assuage. In the dry,

after a dismal wet, we camped by the river, shrunk
to a freshly washed wound. We trolled it a day,
came up empty-handed then abandoned it:
unseasonal rain-clouds wattled the sky and threatened

to bog us in. At the eleven mile dam a scree
of concrete on dark earth, a broken chorus
of shells . Leaving, we stopped to watch
the brown water flow gently under the bridge.

You said, as if you knew, 'Just a minute,
you never know when your last time here will be.'
Two months later, gaunt as a rake, you shook
my hand for the last time: 'See you soon.' And you will.

2. Siege

How dangerous is sentimentality? Enough.
My mother took his reticence for shyness,
the way he would retreat to drink and smoke

outside, or stand behind a door, half an eye
on us, his near relations. Influenced by my mother,
I made the same mistake. Yet he called his brother

'Fat Guts' and each night would cow
his mother, in her 90s, into her chair.
He was a bully, a coward. After his mother died,

he refused to leave her house, turning a gun
on the bailiff before shooting himself in the face.
Years before he'd asked if the book I gave him,

The Best Hated Man in Australia was a gift,
or something else. I had said it was,
but now I know that it was something else.

3. Kerosene

You knew what it was like to return home
to gutters filled with kerosene;

to be raped with the door ajar
while your mother-in-law listened from the other room;

to have watched your daughter
crawl through the legs of her uncles

while your husband inched towards the day
he would father his own grandson.

Now there is more than a continent between us
and much less. At least your ex had the decency

to blow his head off in his car, leaving you
to be whittled away by years.

A part of me is buried with you, the five year-old
tiredly trudging after his beautiful cousin

across the Bridge.

In Memory of Ross Hannaford

Sixteen months before he died I saw him play
at The Red Wheelbarrow
in orange jeans and an orange silk shirt,
just a guitar and a delay,
feeding little riffs into it
until he'd hit a groove which he'd then overlay
with improvisations. In the narrow
room he seemed like a tiger caged behind sixteen repeating bars
every few minutes kicking his left leg out
as he finished a phrase or wobbled the tremolo arm,
his big black sandal almost hitting my knee
then retracting, and playing on with that goose neck bobble
I remembered from *GTK*
when I was six, watching Daddy Cool
play 'Eagle Rock' in a milk bar,
but instead of that plastic lifesaver's cap with a propeller on top
he wore an orange beanie to match his cool jeans.

It's strange how music is a form of time travel
which prophesises, punts us into the past. I learned to dance
with the daughter of the co-founder of One Nation
(not that I knew that then,
only that Anne, with her twin sister, had just arrived
from Adelaide already knowing the steps,
elegant, sophisticated, blonde and aloof).
It was the summer of 1977, my last year of primary
and 'Eagle Rock' was the stop-start soundtrack
to learning how to lead and dosey-doe.
Later we became friends: she sang in my band,

but her sister Debbie was another matter.
Once, when we were studying *Lord of the Flies*
our teacher had us imagine a scenario
in which we were Piggy, Simon, and 'friends':
how should we not end up killing each other?
In my Dudley Do-right way I suggested
some sort of toastmasterly democracy
a benign formality, naively trusting in 'rules'
but Debbie's response was fierce, her black curls shaking:
persecution follows from organization
as night follows day: no one was going to boss her around.

There were less than twenty of us at the gig.
When we stepped out into the warm November air
of Lygon Street, Ross was there, the smoke from his rollie
dissolving into the summery dark,
waiting to thank us for coming to hear him
as if we were friends at a private party
and not itinerant strangers about to part.

Ando at the Sando

i.m. Andrew Robert Bruce Davies (1965-2024)

Then you weren't, suddenly, as usual,
mid-pool game, schooner at low tide,
having phantomed into the slippy night
before the traffic thinned and clouds edged out
the dwindling stars. Now you've vanished
finally, without return: we're left
with your guffaw; that rebound shot in pool
we named after you; the gently iron grip
of your hand in greeting. I'll miss the way
you missed me the last time that we met,
your brokenness strength. Go, friend,
may your gambit with eternity return
to us your warm solidity, the hurt glint
of your unangry heart, your final class turn.

The Poet's Wake

After the dry-eyed service, the wake.
Widow-paced, the mourners wander
down weathered and grass-rent bitumen
from the chapel to the oyster vendor's yard
where plates of them are laid out, seminiferously plump,
with curled and ruddy prawns.

Ripples speak softly against the wall,
an array of imperfections, as if from a dark refractor,
spreading gradually across the river.

The wake is a murmuration of feeding
and remembrance, oyster-eyed widows
on point, and those hierarchies of poets,
assembling and dissolving
before the ebbing tide,
deliver on the afternoon's promise
of continuance and communion.

Minutes after my son was born
I trembled as I cut his umbilical cord
and realized I could no longer judge another,
not at this setting out
from the improvised jetty of thought
over dimples and furrows
and slant serrations of light
on that river of the imagination.
Who else, in setting forth,
should say what shouldn't happen?

Banks of mud slowly rise from this ancestral river,
dark caramel and pocked
by little dark holes which lead to
the nothing out of which we arise
and into which we return,
and out of them comes a crab army
as if created from the act of seeing,
clattering up and sideways, feeding, fending,
translating themselves across pools and mud,
and brandishing their pincers as if defiant.

Beyond them, across the river's cool ebbing
and umber mud, the mirrored shabbiness of mangroves
and, just visible, their pneumatophores
like fingers rising up from underground
which, when stepped on, spring back again,
                                                alive.

Halfway Things

i.m. Jordie Albiston (1961-2022)

On the outer reaches   drifting
where the summer sharpens
pacific glare on its own winnowing
currents   wavery graft of blades
strewn in prismatic deep   bladderwrack
on scripted foam deep in blue-green
homeward   resuming lime and lemon light
of tide

•

Had you never left
you'd be just here in the middle   yep
aslant and at a remove
but time has hoovered you up   yep
up and out into the cosmos.

•

This is the good place, of grass
plumping with rain, and liquidambar
seed pods like meteors burrowed by moonworms,
pebbly clay trickling with the slow runoff
of wind conducting the skitter-chorus of leaves,
suspiring pigface and gold-tipped orb-weavers
patiently cruciform   wasps embossing the leeward hollows
of dune-bedded rocks:
there is no other place, just places,
none better than this place, where you aren't.

Halfway things. Echo and abandon,
low stratus mizzling imperfection:
                              out of the horizon
of mortal thoughts, light disappears
into mottled yolk, livid-veined and bluish orisons
of refracted darkness. Slab-cold
wind picks off the defenceless spume.
Something older than fire
that inhabits all things at their core
leans into its work, a spoor
of damaged shapes, forgetful
that today is deeper than yesterday
but still as shallow as a shimmering puddle,
weird as a truckful of dewy-eyed camels
chewing sideways as they wobble over the bridge
at Waratah Station.

·

unspeakable joy   unspeakable
grief irrupts playfully   prolonging
itself   recalcitrant   rosaceous
clouds and the sun's disappearing self,
into nights that seem more permanent now,
more like a state of affairs arrived at
and agreed to   even announced as angles
of carpentry   mortice of coffin-boards,
dead flowers for the dead, flowering once more.

DIAL 0, OK?

Parthenope

Sick of being an ending, Death decides to become a he.
He wants his portrait hung in the Archibald,
and he wants to be liked. He picks a fight
with Sin and wins. He pays a genealogist
to confect him a family tree. It begins with
paramecium and ends with paracetamol.
His second cousin is a cetacean
who has a wooden leg. That's not right,
thinks Death, a cetacean doesn't have legs.
What's it like to come home, he wonders,
and find the fridge is filled with Ratsak?
He goes home. The fridge is filled with Ratsak.
Imperceptibly, he acquires the habits of a lifetime
spent alone at a laminex table, playing cards.
That one, the Ace of Spades, keeps coming up
on top. He'd prefer the Queen of Hearts
but her face is a möbius strip, her eyes
red carnelians. He goes to the window,
watching water vein the glass and a lonely parachute
dwindle to a mushroom over the fields.
No one warned him about his waning appetite
and what goes with it. What if you urinate ink
in quarantine? There you go, he says
to himself, at it again. He reconsiders outsourcing
his core business: an avid diva
glares from his screen, triumphantly
announcing her hostile takeover. Game on.

The Excursion

You rose at dawn and shaved the light into your face.
The mirror occluded with fawning steam
your planed face somewhere behind it.

Outside tentative rain began pattering,
sounding like an ageing mother shuffling up a hall.
The downpipe puttered with echoes of sky.

Mortal glottals. You could not stay inside
so you set out, sole to glistening footpath.
In the long light of spring you were young again.

You followed the wet path between rat run
traffic and mouldering pastel terraces, took unknown streets
hoping to arrive nowhere. Now you are invisible.

A pair of windows paned with grey light
put you in mind of Michael Caine who once said,
'if I keep blinking, it weakens me, but if I'm talking to you

and I don't blink, and I just keep going
and I don't blink, and I keep on going
and I don't blink, and I just keep going...'

your eyes began to itch as you hear him saying
how it makes him a very strong person.
You had entered the song of unfamiliar suburbs,

their fitful maze, their chock-a-block
and dreary dreams of the Anthropocene.
In these new streets, incidental shimmers

of tar and yaps of territory shunted you
towards the harbour, where domestic interiors
narrowed the view until you found yourself

on a girdered walk across a bridge. On the other side,
a tiny green with she-oaks, a cul de sac
with a thicketed verge and a path through it

into a field that rolled up a hill to a fence.
Just out of earshot and over the page,
people. In the middle of the field, a pile of limbs,

detritus of an inside thrown out, boxes,
twigs, a doll with lidless, rolled back eyes
crackling in a blaze. Soon a crowd of onlookers gather.

You avoid their accusatory stares, and climb
the grunching cyclone wire. Say nothing.
Just keep going, and don't blink.

Dynamics of Reason

This poem is down on all fours rooting
through rubbish. You might call it hunkering
but I call it preparation aforethought:
gather this refuse while you may,
it won't last forever. Don't feed it,
let it make its own way, snuffling
through filth, there's a jewel in there somewhere.

There's a jewel in there somewhere, a rose
blooming in winter, a marlinspike
hitched to a moonsheep's fetlock,
a tail wagging a dog. If it was up
to me, there'd be a chorizo on the horizon,
rhyming with it, or overlapping it like a sign.

Overlapping it like a sign, the new ambition
is to pencil in 'Westfield sublime'
for our interior vertiginousness.
There is no bottom to which we might plunge,
only an Andean space that opens as far
as the distances between us, mulga
hanzi magotting on a plain.

Magotting on a plain the poem reels
the sunset in, destroying time, the milkshakes
of its stoned youth. It goes on rooting,
throwing out refractions, ampersands, shucking
barrows, perspiring in a welter of words,
the kind that keeps on nuttering, nickering.

Monotudes

I was at the collapse of the Odradek stadium.

Dysphoric plane tree fluff filled the air.

Dodmans sieved the lettuce, sputnik-eared.

A curlew in a coracle afloat on the canal.

By the ruins at curfew a police horse caracoles.

Tattoo the evening dark with mottled lips.

Slip between the cracks of other tongues.

Don't forget the charger, bring it with you.

For light read only habit, heavenly glow.

There's an app which names the stars and constellations.

Castanets and finger cymbals packed into a box.

Excursions after dark require less planning.

Voice is aural phloem or formal air.

For air read what you signed up for tomorrow.

I don't know why I have so little time.

Constant Trembling

I wrote to President Roosevelt since they were doing what they
smoked and I began perfumed operations on the young.
There was even a dominant finch undergoing several changes
and subjected to various kinds of America in a nine-passenger
station-wagon, pretending to be pirates and shown much of Tiger Tim.
Incendiary bombs were initially long and intensive.
Young punks, self-confident and easy-going, infected me
with an odd mixture of individuality: a name trimmed with others.
Little children contented themselves with raccoons, their shoulders
lovely as girls with flowers. A sense of Divine beauty
makes one atomic bomb a month, which did not improve
my appearance, white shirt and leather trousers
walking backwards up a hill. The universal is animated
by people, including Vietnam veterans, who said they could tell
when a girl had lost her isotope separation plant behind those songs
which dramatize Paris, in which handsome girls and rich men
trade their virginity. We stood around the enclosure
and recorded over several nights at CBGB some who spoke in well-bred voices,
the obvious analogy being with music. Then, naked as the moon, we danced
in other cities. The scenes then did the same. We went up the yard
forming in front of an audience of friends who would also adopt, for a while,
a yellow hare, a relation of the garden, the garden of gelatinous moonlight
and a sense of something evil.

Shy Architecture

There is no jewel hidden
inside the box, but an inside
hidden within the box.
I open it and the light
slants in like a prism
of unknowing on
the nothing that is hidden.

It is like the human heart
considered as a midden
of lost bivalves: whole pairs
joined at a tangent of love,
sundered halves reunited
or kept apart. This nothing
which is something at its core.

The darkness hidden within
accentual light strums
the grand fringe of knowing
as gentian evenings drain
the sky of tenderness.
Something is still inside
the box, a self folded

into a shy architecture
of corners pleated, crimped
and cabined into walls
inside of which is nothing
but the colour and texture of screens.

I approach this empty prison
from my little patch of outside

where the wind is herringbone
filled with cries of squabbling
birds. I'll be as far
as near to the vanishing light
which folds upon itself
and darkens slowly with
the terrible weight of arrival.

KOOL-AID DISPENSERS

The Dawson Twins

Our class was the pool into which they gazed
at themselves, occasionally summoning one of us
from PE class, my cousin perhaps, for a quick fuck
in the mat room. How badly it all turned out,
although the Department of Education took their time
disbanding that ring of theirs only years after
one of their wives went 'missing'. I don't miss them,
nor do I like seeing them as they are now,
bald, scorned, troublingly untroubled,
pushing preposterous lies about their innocence
with an ageing, mendacious insistence
that somehow they had never, couldn't, didn't.
On the other side of their Adonic reflections:
their loveless selves, the nadir of perfection.

Achtung Baby

In Year 9 German a future Miss Australia
used to comment on the bent of my genitalia.
'Rick's leaning to the right again,' she'd say
as the class repeated, 'es tut mir sehr weh.'

I Make Northrop Frye Laugh, 1986

I might have been part-way through *Fearful Symmetry*
or yet to start when I entertained the hope
that at twenty I might make Northrop Frye
laugh when I told him I'd read Locke's *Rape of the Pope*.

Ode to the Manifest Image

found poem from G.E. Moore

There exists at present a living human body.
Mine. This body was born at a certain time
in the past, and has existed continuously
ever since, though not without undergoing changes.
It was much smaller when it was born.
Ever since, it has been either in contact
with or not far from the surface of the earth.
At every moment since it was born,
there have also existed many other things, having shape
and size in three dimensions (in the same familiar sense
in which it has), from which it has been at various distances
(in the familiar sense in which it is now at a distance
both from that mantelpiece and from that bookcase,
and at a greater distance from the bookcase than it is
from the mantelpiece); also there have (very often,
at all events) existed some other things of this kind
with which it was in contact (in the familiar sense
in which it is now in contact with the pen I am holding
in my right hand and with some of the clothes I am wearing).
Among the things which have, in this sense, formed
part of its environment (i.e., have been either
in contact with it, or at some distance from it,
however great) there have, at every moment
since its birth, been large numbers of other
living human bodies, each of which
has, like it, at some time been born,
continued to exist from some time after birth,
been, at every moment of its life

after birth, either in contact with
or not far from the surface of the earth;
and many of these bodies have already
died and ceased to exist. But the earth had existed
also for many years before my body
was born; and for many of these years,
also, large numbers of human bodies
had, at every moment, been alive
upon it; and many of these bodies had died
and ceased to exist before it was born.
Finally (to come to a different class of propositions),
I am a human being, and I have,
at different times since my body was born,
had many different experiences, of each
of many different kinds: I have often perceived
both my own body and other things
which formed part of its environment,
including other human bodies; I have
not only perceived things of this kind, but have also
observed facts about them, such as, for instance,
the fact which I am now observing, that
that mantelpiece is at present nearer to my body
than that bookcase; I have been aware
of other facts, which I was not at the time
observing, such as, for instance, the fact, of which
I am now aware, that my body existed yesterday
and was then also for some time nearer to that
mantelpiece than to that bookcase; I have
had expectations with regard to the future,
and many beliefs of other kinds, both true
and false; I have thought of imaginary things
and persons and incidents, in the reality of which

I did not believe; I have had dreams;
and I have had feelings of many different kinds.
And, just as my body has been the body of a human
being, namely myself, who has, during
his lifetime, had many experiences of each
of these (and other) different kinds; so,
in the case of very many of the other
human bodies which have lived upon the earth,
each has been the body of a different
human being, who has, during the lifetime
of that body, had many different experiences
of each of these (and other) different kinds.

The Earth

Contrary to popular belief, I peaked in the plasticene era
when I was able to assume many different forms.
I was much larger when I was born
but forceps were not necessary. Slowly, by degrees
I warmed to the idea of myself
as a necessary form. I continue to endure
a kind of igneous acne, and I bathe
in pulsative oceans. My winds
weave the elements invisibly, people
keep on popping up and popping off
at all times of my days, yet if I turn
to face you, it is not because of interest,
but turning, and turning, is simply what I do.

The Answer

1. Chidley's Travelling Dark Room, 1875

After her stroke, my mother sat in an easy chair
suspended by india-rubber bands from the roof
of the travelling dark room. In summer
on level roads she enjoyed the scenery
but in winter on uneven roads she screamed.

I had gone to Father in Ararat to learn photography.
Chidley's Travelling Dark Room was like a gipsy caravan
but larger, with steps leading up to a waiting room.
There was also a dark room and, at the end,
a large room covered in glass in which

the camera sat upon a tripod, cowled
like someone condemned. On the walls
hung the worthies of Beveridge, Benalla, Violet Town,
albumenized by my father, wives standing
half a step behind their rigid, seated husbands.

I could see an indescribable gleam in their eyes.
Among them, under a beeswax sheen,
was an albumen print of a slippered pugilist
just after his defeat of Isaiah 'Wild' Wright
over sixteen rounds of bare-knuckle boxing at Beechworth.
I noticed his head was smaller than average,
his monobrow and two cruel eyes drawn close
like raisins kneaded together in dough.

Around this time I perfected that technique,
applied to myself, I'd seen in a French pack of cards.
I suffered from alternating moods:
a strange sense of waking in the bush near Beveridge,
like veils lifting from the straggly gums and ministered fields,
and sunlight entering directly into my blood.
Then there were days when the same landscape
sank into the mundane, under an unfamiliar cloud.
I was melancholy, but later seized by an odd hilarity.
One day I saw a pansy in a cottage garden
which gave me the true 'Divine Joy'.
There had *never* been such a pansy as this one!
It urged a remembrance in me
of those blunt flashes of revelation,
of waking to the unearthly glow of the infinite present.

After my mother had her final stroke,
she was washed and two pennies placed on her eyes.
The bed bugs that had been under her had fled.
I felt a desire to laugh.
When the coffin came, just a few boards nailed together,
I carried it in and said, 'Here, old woman, is your coffin'.

2. Gravity

My earliest memory: a child in petticoats
and a well in the middle of a field.
The child disappears, bringing Father running across the brightness
to the dark plummeting core of the world.
I go on playing, indifferent to their fates.

I remember sailing into Port Phillip. A friend
of Father's, Mr. Moody, came out on a boat to meet us.
By a strange chance I burst into tears on seeing his son Walter.
Later, we would lie together and receive what he called 'comfort'
by sucking each other's penis. Poor Walter, dead at eighteen!

A younger brother of Walter's used to sit in the summer-house
with his member erect and extended, grossly,
considering his age. I remember his satyr-face,
laughing with tears in his eyes at his sisters' astonishment.
Eventually his mother had his night-shirt sewn up.

One day at the Brunswick Street boarding school I was surprised
to glimpse in the next room our teacher,
a young man chalking the end of his cock,
which was erect and bulging out of his trousers,
for the amusement of someone I could not see.

That night in his bedroom I asked him what a woman's privates
were like. A look of shame crossed his face.
Not knowing what to do, I put my hand under his gown
and took hold of his cock, and then he put his effeminate hand
under my gown and rubbed up and down.
I lay still as death, one second lifted into clouds,
buried miles deep at another – carried along
by an entirely new excitement.
This, then was the meaning of those inherited longings
that had come at intervals, almost as far back as I could remember
like the veil that lifted outside Beveridge
or the divinity in that little pansy,
my rage at a better-dressed boy,
or the need I had to slam my member with a toilet seat
so that it turned black and they said, 'Chidley's got a black cock'.

3. The Law of Ugliness

My first connection was with a middle-aged woman,
not at all handsome. She would not let me look:
'It's quite good enough for you, young shaver'.
She made horrid faces and groaned.
I must have hurt her. That night turned closer and darker.

It took years of all kinds of connection
in all kinds of places: in Fitzroy Park
or on the sand, like a dog licking
a woman in a lane, before I realized
the injuries caused by the shock of coition.

I saw it most closely in Ada.
When we first met she had spurned-spaniel eyes
and a delicate cameo face,
level brow like Ruskin's infinite curve,
ever approaching but never attaining a straight line.
But after connection, her eyes became less clear
her brow would knit and her eyebrows thicken.
On one occasion she frowned stiff,
her hands clenched and turned in
with the strength of ten, frothing at the mouth.
How brassy and unreal everything was after connection.
I became sulky and bear-like, overcome by murderous moods,
ratty, my brain adhering to the back of my skull,
viler than any man who had ever lived.

I had seen it before, in the face of the boxer, Ned Kelly,
in portraits of Sir George Reid, and Edward VII:
the accumulated shocks of unnatural coition,

the injured eyes, the wasted jawbone, the vanity
of an involuted face, the fixed frown.

A sheet of albumen paper placed upon a table
will curl inwards from both ends, forming two scrolls
which touch at a point, exactly like the midpoint of two damaged eyes
in a forehead turned in on itself through the shocks of unnatural coition.

Whenever I was addicted to tampering,
my perverted character disfigured my hands and nails,
made my eyes smaller and shrunk my head;
In every ugly and contracted muscle, injured iris, frowning brow,
pigeon-toes, knock-knees, bent back, bow legs,
round, narrow forehead, head like a wizened apple:
everything converged, even thought,
a convergence of ends which is the law of ugliness.

4. The Answer

I am writing in a hot and close room over a lane
in which men cart bleeding and stinking skins all day.
My landlord, a musician, goes in so heavily for coition
he is always having epileptic fits, often out of his mind.
Under the thin skull of his bald head
I can see his brain squirming about.
There is no compromise with vice.
Walking the streets, people I pass talk about me,
I am sure, as the man who will reform the world.

Once, when lying with Ada in a close embrace,
my flaccid penis found its way
into her vagina. This was natural coition
because we loved each other,
the manner of love in the unfallen state:
I have seen a monkey put her hand
between her legs and hold her mate's penis
to her vulva, and nothing come of it.
Monkeys never have erections.
An entire does not force an entrance
to the mare, but rather waits until her vulva winks.
There are no straight lines in nature,
whereas an erect penis is quite straight;
it is an *ugly* thing, and we are all ashamed of it.

In Spring lovers should feed on fragrant, electric fruit
so that their skins will have a bloom
like the last touch of the sun on a peach.
One kiss shall lead to another at natural intervals
and with a rising intensity, their kisses
increase in joy until their mouths cling
and their teeth meet gently. They will inhale
from each other's lungs, their navels cup
with magnetic thrills, as her young vagina becomes erect
and waits until in that fusing embrace
his unerect penis shall touch her clitoris,
her vagina flash open and suck it in
by pressure of air and secured by its head
at each step by the rugae of her vagina,
and then their whole bodies will melt in ecstacy.

Our evolution is not yet complete, and its next surprise
will be that we shall float in the air in Paradise
without need for clothes, not even in winter.
We are still at the bottom of our sea, but some day,
when we have recovered from our fall
we shall become lighter until we can levitate freely
and then young lovers in the season will meet
in the azure above the Spring blossoms and couple there.

The History of Violence

The history of violence is very brief.
It begins with one protozoa ingesting another,
trees clutching the earth, birds wrangling
within them, and doesn't end
with the riddle of royalty, decapitations, gangs,
or poets guilted into one mode
over another. Some of them turn away
from their squabbles towards the relative infinitude
of light. Has it always existed? Can it be said
to have always burned as the nation of violence
eternal blazes like a star above us?

KOELS TO NEWCASTLE

Five Puddles

This one is an eye
glaucous with cloud,

that one is a tremor
of longing for the sea;

beyond them is the umbo
of the quincuncial whole,

the crown of a shivering
eucalypt edges a neighbour

and the last one bleeds
in surrender to its emblem,

the rampant hero
Jingxi, in gumboots.

Milk Teeth

They start out nervously raising palisades
from bleeding roots, white-cored snubs
picketing growing determination:
let them arrange themselves
in a parliament of white enamel,
rows of antic fluorescence
in a crowd-sourced mouth.
When their time is up, the whole punk
insurrection trades itself in
for a nip of immortality.

Walking with my young son I remember I am only a year shy of the age my father was when he had his fatal stroke

1.

You know how to disband
the iron clouds holding the sky fast.
It disbelieves in endings,
beguiles the pandanus, cycads and gums
swaying through the afternoon.
Will the edge of the wind
sharpen itself on my roof again?
There's a silence underneath the rocks
and violence in drifting shadow
inevitable as the shape
a cruising shark inhabits.

2.

Confederates of the sun, browsing bees
hum on the jasmine hedge,
filling out their yellow jodhpurs.
Somehow a library has spilled its guts
outside, a tercet of books
beside two hollowed hemispheres of watermelon.
Spring arrives in a heatwave —
grasshoppers the size of small rodents
nibble neat crescents in the frangipani.
A sunshower strolls across the lawn.

3.

Cold winds and a primal sun
scream through the park.
The Styx is full but devoid of fish
and brownly rippling two white ducks
and a multitude of fluid generalizations:
my son is angry with a ball, but scared
of a big white dog who wants to play
but possibly wants to bite him too.
Old school birds terrorise the trees.
The audacity of whatever he wants –
too much presence, not enough rhetoric?
Let's tell the mullet and rats nothing.
The grass won't leave the dirt unwritten,
the children swing, snottily determined.

苏轼《洗儿诗》

人皆養子望聰明，
我被聰明誤一生；
惟願孩子愚且魯，
無災無難到公卿。

Su Shi 'Washing my Son'

Everyone hopes their child will grow up intelligent,
but since intelligence has only ruined my life,
I just wish that my son be foolish and ignorant;
then without any trouble he'll become a cabinet minister.

Arborealism

Palings, around a sapling
thin as a wrist, bent back
by the wind, joined by wire
and forming a raggedy pentagon,
are spare and obtuse, listing
in tune with their younger cousin,
willing their planed forms free.

Kooragang Dawn

The cool might of morning
deposes the night casually, like a government
that falls at a by-election as a trawler returns,
darkness dripping from its nets.
Out on the northern arm, a broadening wake
of dawn: a pair of white-faced herons pick
among the pigface, nacreous
pinks ripple with ochre and russet.
The trawler skirts the mangroves
in a bright wake which smooths
into level icing. Soon the mass
of water rhymes with the sky, then veers
into its own fractured thrall
as a brahminy kite thermals the gathering sun.

Warabrook Wetlands

It's August, cold at the temples.
I walk home indirectly
    over the footbridge traversing wetlands and railway
    each railing like a tyre-iron
and under each path light
    a loosening gyre of midges

The sky is a sodden gauze of darkening grey,
        and at the horizon, low stratus
    dusted with yellow toner
Wandering whistle-duck dive and paddle
in the pewter waters past the rail line
and to my right, a pair of kingfishers cartwheel through a tree
and settle in détente   squawking

I walked this way the week before in relative darkness
    below I can now still discern multifoliate sway
of tressed greenery   elephant's ears
an organized overlay and folding sharp edges
vanish under and over each other without reason
    or too much of it

Shovelers and grey teal dot the slate water
a clear breeze combs swamp-fern imperceptibly
velvet knotweed   pale smartweed   curled dock
lesser joyweed   purple-loosestrife   mudmat
creeping sneezeweed   water pennyworts   dollar weed
    each leaf pointing to another
        so diversely   there is a density

of different kinds of fold:
    pleat and rhyme   remembrance   overlay
yield   déjà vu   and forgetfulness
    and next week will be lighter

Food Poisoning, Red Rooster, Waratah

For a while there I was a shivering klein bottle
vesuviating at both ends: stepmother's breath
at the bone. Delirium, a country made of numbers
never fitting, prime bleeding night into dawn
then back again. That yawning catechism
of failed equations, fatigue that marched on and on
on numbly numbered feet around a planet
ringed by a sense of my irrelevance,
its plethora of moons my jack-in-the-box thoughts.
After my inside had become an outside,
my peloton of worry came to rest
at the foot of the mountain, the centre of my grumpiverse
which I began to slowly climb again.

Three pigeons

I watch three pigeons stutter-strutting the vacant lot
    next to the repurposed church in the Inner West.
One follows another who mirrors the first. Is it
    habit or superstition that makes something
circular of this triadic claque of wings, like
    oil on seawater throwing colours off its
bobbling surface, rolling from a purple sheen to
    green and back again? Sometimes days like these fly
into my eye, an exclamation of multitasking
    sunshine marshalling the bright walls. One pigeon
hops, another spreads his wings carnally, and like
    the third way in an argument, the last one ebbs
and pecks, but can't evade the revolving syllogism
    of their walk. A screen without edges bathes us
in its blue: those aren't clouds, but systems
    shepherding the day across the sky.

Koels to Newcastle

If you're not living in Sydney you're really camping
— Paul Keating

I come back from the valley
to that too familiar funk — malls
that are the reason, housing an excuse
and the trees that come alive at four a.m.
with plangent call after call. The koels come home
to call the summer in,
just like the coal which leaves here
to arc up oceans, dial up the globe.
This morning I woke to a little inland sea
covering half the road, my neighbour's house opposite
rippling upside-down in its shallows:
burst water main. She's leaning, within cooee on her gate:
"It usually costs a bundle for a waterfront view."

Jingxitude

Why was the wine drunk?
Because it wanted to be human.

How I love thunderstorms:

the way, before their bickering flashes start,
the presaging tang of petrichor
seeps in through the front door
humidly tinged with box and chlorophyll.
And when it starts it is with the thrill
of the cosmic on a domestic scale:
snipes and spars that rend and boom,
sheets of light that leap into the night sky
illuminating our snug insignificance.

Notes

'给京禧'：to Jingxi (my son).

'In Memory of Ross Hannaford': David Ettridge is the co-founder of One Nation to whom the poem refers.

苏轼（Sū Shì 1037-1101），also known as 苏东坡 (Sū Dōngpō) was a Song dynasty statesman and poet who endured exile a number of times.

'The Dawson Twins': Chris and Paul Dawson played first grade rugby league for the Newtown Jets in the 1970s. Paul was my PE teacher at Forest High School, Chris taught at nearby Cromer High School. In 2022 Chris Dawson was found guilty of the murder in 1982 of his wife Lynette. In 2023 my 3rd cousin and classmate Shelley Oates-Wilding told *Sixty Minutes* that she had been in a sexual relationship with Paul Dawson while we were at high school, their liaisons often occurring during our PE classes. According to Shelley, Paul ended their relationship shortly after his brother's wife went missing.

'Achtung Baby': the beauty queen in question is Tracey Dale.

'I Make Northrop Frye Laugh, 1986': Northrop Frye actually laughed at this joke at St. Paul's College, Sydney University, in 1986.

'Walking with my young son I remember I am only a year shy of the age my father was when he had his fatal stroke': 'The Styx' is the name of a creek running through Newcastle.

Jordie Albiston (1961-2022) was a great Australian poet. She was my friend and I published four of her books. Her sudden death was a terrible loss for Australian poetry.

Acknowledgements

I would like to thank Dael Allison, Gillian Barlow, Judith Beveridge, Ken Bolton, Julie Chevalier, Martin Dolan, Linda Godfrey, Hilary Hewitt, Carol Jenkins, Peter Kirkpatrick, Anthony Lawrence, John Leonard, Jacinta Le Plastrier, Greg McLaren, Catherine McGrath, Mal McKimmie, Gail Nason, Todd Turner and John Watson for their reading, edits and suggestions. Thanks to Shane Strange for publishing this book.

'Ode to the Manifest Image' is largely a found poem, a versification of a section of G.E. Moore's 'A Defence of Common Sense' in his *Selected Writings* (London: Routledge, 1993). This poem was first published in my article "Show don't tell': What Creative Writing has to teach Philosophy', published in *Philosophies* special issue 'Poetry and Ordinary Language' (*Philosophies* 2024, *9*(5), 150; https://doi.org/10.3390/philosophies9050150 https://www.mdpi.com/2409-9287/9/5/150).

An earlier version of 'Letter to a Dead Parent' was first published in my *Selected Poems* (Maida Vale: Eyewear, 2021) and a manuscript of it is stored in The Durham Archive as part of The Mary Midgley Biscuit Tin project.

The three poems that comprise 'Western Elegies: three ways home', as well as 'In Memory of Ross Hannaford' and 'Halfway Things' were previously published as 'Five Elegies' in *The Anabranch: Newcastle Poetry Prize Anthology 2022*, and were awarded the local prize in 2022.

'Three Pigeons' was originally published in *The Book of Birds*, edited by Penelope Layland & Lesley Lebkowicz (Canberra: Recent Work, 2023).

'The Answer' is adapted from: *The Confessions of William James Chidley*, Ed. S. McInerney, (St Lucia: UQP, 1977); William Chidley, *The Answer*, (Sydney: Sydney D. Smith, 1915); and William Chidley, *The Answer*, (Pyrmont: W.J. Chidley, 1912). The wording closely echoes Chidley's style in the originals.

About the Author

A melancholy figure on the lonely windswept streets of Newcastle, David Musgrave occasionally emerges from his habitual funk to write books of poems, of which this is his tenth. Often he claims to be wandering to and from the University of Newcastle, where he teaches creative writing. At other times he desultorily discharges his duties at the independent publishing house Puncher & Wattmann, which he founded in 2003. In his spare time he translates classical Chinese poetry and ferries his son around to his (Jingxi's, that is) many interesting extra-curricular activities, deriving further poems from his son's perceptive observations.

www.ingramcontent.com/pod-product-compliance
Lightning Source LLC
Chambersburg PA
CBHW030317100526
44585CB00014BA/944